Holy Luck

Holy Luck

Poems

Eugene H. Peterson

William B. Eerdmans Publishing Company
Grand Rapids, Michigan / Cambridge, U.K.

Eerdmans 10/2013
$12.00

Published 2013 by
Wm. B. Eerdmans Publishing Co.
2140 Oak Industrial Drive N.E., Grand Rapids, Michigan 49505 /
P.O. Box 163, Cambridge CB3 9PU U.K.

Printed in the United States of America

19 18 17 16 15 14 13   7 6 5 4 3 2 1

Library of Congress Cataloging-in-Publication Data

Peterson, Eugene H., 1932-
[Poems. Selections]
Holy luck: poems / Eugene H. Peterson.
    pages   cm
    ISBN 978-0-8028-7099-5 (pbk.: alk. paper)
    1. Christian poetry, American.   I. Title.

PS3566.E7685A6   2013
811'.54 — dc23

2013021224

www.eerdmans.com

For Jan, in our 55th year of marriage

Contents

Introduction

David's Psalms were my introduction to poetry. I was thirteen years old and had just purchased with my own money a burgundy, leather-bound King James Bible. It was summer and we had just moved across town to a neighborhood where I had yet to make new friends. Friendless and bored, I filled in the empty, unfriended days by reading my new Bible. It wasn't long before I discovered the Psalms.

The biblical culture in which I grew up was fiercely insistent that every word in the Bible is true just as it appears on the page, literally true, straight from the mouth of God, no questions asked. But in the Psalms that way of reading wasn't getting me anywhere I wanted to go. I read ". . . thou, O Lord, art a shield. . . . The Lord is my rock. . . . put thou my tears in thy bottle. . . . God shall shoot at them with an arrow. . . ."

God is a weapon? God is a rock? God carries a specimen bottle to collect tears? God prowls the earth with bow and arrow to destroy my enemies?

Literal wasn't working for me. But I was shy about asking questions, fearful that I would be reprimanded for calling the

Bible, God's very words, into question. In the church world I inhabited asking questions was suspect and so I plodded on, quite enjoying the rhythms and images but puzzled how to make literal sense of them. And in the process of plodding, without really noticing what was happening, I quit trying to figure these psalms out and found myself drawn into a world of words in which I was no longer a questioner but a participant, and enjoying the participation.

About halfway through the summer I realized that there was a way of using words that was not literal. I was learning more or less on the job the magic of metaphor, although it would be years before I acquired a vocabulary to name what I was experiencing in David's poems. Language began to explode with possibilities. There was a lot more to using words than making shopping lists, giving directions to a lost stranger looking for a street address, memorizing dates and names in preparation for passing exams, calling my dog, proving the existence of God. Far more was involved in the language that David was using than dictionary definitions. Sounds and combinations of sound were part of it, rhythm and repetition and rhyme. I found myself not so much looking for facts that I could use but participating in the making of something true or beautiful or compelling.

By the end of the summer I had added Isaiah and Jesus and Paul to my stable of poets and after a few years managed to seek out Emily Dickinson, George Herbert, T. S. Eliot, Gerard Manley Hopkins, William Carlos Williams, Denise Levertov, Luci Shaw, Scott Cairns and their friends as allies; but it was David who got me started.

I had learned that poets are caretakers of language, shepherds of words, protecting them from desecration, exploitation, misuse. Words not only mean something, they are something, each with a sound and rhythm all its own. Poets are not primarily trying to tell us or get us to do something. A poet uses words not to explain or describe but make. Poet *(poetes)* means "maker." By attending to words with playful discipline (or disciplined playfulness) I am drawn into deeper respect both for the words themselves and the reality they invite me into. I do not have more information after reading a poem; I have more experience.

By the time I embraced my vocational identity as a pastor I had realized that pastors and poets have a lot in common: we use words with reverence, get immersed in everyday particulars, are wary of abstractions, spy out the glories of the commonplace, warn of illusions, attend to the subtle interconnections between rhythm and meaning and spirit. I found it significant that the biblical prophets and psalmists were all poets and that they provided me with congenial company for integrating my own prophetic and psalmic work, my preaching and praying.

Day-by-day pastoral work seems in the actual doing of it mostly improvisation. Is there nothing solid to build upon? As I looked around in those early years what I observed to my dismay was that the prevailing pastoral practice was mostly built on sand, the sands shifting every few years. The big truths — God, kingdom, salvation, justice, soul, sin, forgiveness, worship, compassion — were politely acknowledged but then thinly veneered with the trappings of a depersonalizing and secularizing American culture. The big "truths" didn't seem to have much to do with social relations, business practices, and political positions in the everyday "between Sundays" ways in which the people I was working with took up with the world. I began asking the question, "But how does this work on the ground?" With poets training my imagination I started noticing stones all over the place, cornerstones and keystones, stones that "the builders rejected." Rejected because they were not of size or shape that would command attention and give distinction to what was being built. For the most part these stones were words.

Almost everything the pastor does involves words. I preach and teach, pray and direct, using words. People often pay particular attention to me on the chance that God may be using my words to speak to them. I have a responsibility to use words accurately and well. But it isn't easy. I live in a world where words are used carelessly by some, cunningly by others. It is easy to say carelessly whatever comes to mind, trusting my role as pastor to compensate for my inane speech. It is easy to speak what either flatters or manipulates and so acquire power over others. In a subtle way just being a pastor subjects my words to the possibilities of corruption, reducing the "Word made flesh" to words that advertise Jesus and depersonalize the gospel into abstract "truths" and moralizing clichés. I found that keeping company with poets, men and women who care about words and are honest with them, who respect and honor their sheer overwhelming power, kept me alert — biblically alert, Jesus alert. I left their company less careless, my reverence for words and the Word restored. And from time to time I wrote a poem of my own. The people who read them were almost exclusively friends and family and congregation. A few found their way into a journal or magazine. But all of them were rooted in my pastoral vocation.

I have gathered these poems under three headings, all of them written in the working context of the Kingdom of God: Holy Luck, Rustling Grass, Smooth Stones.

Section I: Holy Luck. Early in my formation as a pastor I realized that I had a very flawed imagination for comprehending what was involved in giving witness to and providing direction for embracing and practicing the Christian life, a holy life. I was bringing together fragments of understanding and experience that had seemed to work for me but as I pursued a pastoral vocation I found that they didn't make much of a dent in the prevailing culture of America, a culture thoroughly secularized and commodified. I went looking for something that could integrate the pieces of my experience into something larger than my experience, something that oriented me in the conditions of Kingdom of God life. At some point early on I hit on the Beatitudes as a place to start. Matthew placed Jesus' Beatitudes at the threshold of his definitive Sermon on the Mount. Jesus' overture to his comprehensive symphony sermon, these eight so-called Beatitudes, insist on a radical renovation of our imaginations as a first step in understanding the Kingdom life that Jesus proclaims in word and deed. Eight conditions or circumstances which we commonly find either hard to accept or difficult to achieve are reinterpreted as basic stuff to be embraced in Kingdom of God living. Everyone who decides to follow Jesus becomes, whether we know it at the outset or not, an apprentice in welcoming these conditions. As we do it we find them quite different than we had supposed.

This strategic placing caught my imagination as also definitive to what I was giving witness to as a pastor. The characteristic quality of each Beatitude is its ruthless and unqualified rejection of the common understanding of what it means to take up with the world and then its replacement of that understanding with a total reorientation of the imagination as we take up with the way followers of Jesus speak and act in the Kingdom of God. I knew it would take awhile and I took my time. But over the period of about seven years I had this sequence of Beatitude poems, Holy Luck, that kept my daily work of witness oriented in the Kingdom that Jesus inaugurated in the world but that was not defined by it. They have served me well as a kind of declaration of independence from the ways of the world.

Section II: The Rustling Grass. My entire life takes place in conditions identified as Kingdom of God, not just my "spiritual" life or my "church" life or my "religious" life, but my entire life. Recognition was incremental, but eventually it was there. And not just my life, but everyone's life. And not just human lives but the entire creation: the good and bad, the beautiful and ugly. And not just people like me but agnostics and Muslims and Buddhists.

Most reality is invisible. There is plenty to be seen and heard and touched and tasted and smelled: a rainbow of colors in flowers and sunsets, a symphony of tunes and melodies, rhythms and accents, textures smooth and rough, flavors sweet and sour, fragrance and stench. But life in the Kingdom is an immersion in a much larger, more comprehensive reality. Most of what I see and hear, smell and touch, I soon discover is an opening, a window or door, to something invisible: beauty, truth, goodness — but not those words as such, not abstractions, nothing quantifiable or measurable. The incarnation ("became flesh and dwelt among us"!) puts us in touch with what cannot be touched.

It didn't take me long to realize that the Scriptures don't speak of the One whom it calls "Lord" in the way we might expect, as a human lord, furnished with authority and power and maintaining and executing his own will. Jesus, in particular, rarely seemed to be recognized as Son of God. He mostly did his work on the sidelines, unnoticed, ignored, or even scorned, without fanfare. I made it my task to pay attention to the ordinary and then identify aspects of the life of salvation and Kingdom matters where I detected them, as in "the rustling grass." I think of them as field notes as Scripture and prayer and happenings come together in this Kingdom of God way of life. Writing a poem, which in our culture at least doesn't get much attention, seemed like a good way to pay attention.

Section III, Smooth Stones, gathers occasional poems that seemed to happen along as I was doing everything else: happenings on Maryland forest trails and Montana mountains, marriage and family, birth and death, being playful with words, digging wells with words. David's "five smooth stones" became a metaphor for discovering significance in every detail encountered while following Jesus.

I couldn't help but notice that the stories of Jesus, the person in whose steps I hoped to be following, were only seldom in synagogue or temple. Most of the time Jesus and those who were following him were walking and talking on Galilean roads, fishing on a Galilean sea, having meals with friends and sometimes enemies (or at least people who held him in suspicion), touching lepers, being touched by women. I was learning to keep my eyes open. I didn't want to miss a thing. A friend wrote a book with the title, "God Hides in Plain Sight." That seems to me right.

I. Holy Luck

"Good luck have thou with thine honour."

PSALM 45:4 (BOOK OF COMMON PRAYER)

The Lucky Poor

"Blessed are the poor in spirit"

A beech tree in winter, white
Intricacies unconcealed
Against sky blue and billowed
Clouds, carries in its emptiness
Ripeness: sap ready to rise
On signal, buds alert to burst
To leaf. And then after a season
Of summer a lean ring to remember
The lush fulfilled promises.
Empty again in wise poverty
That lets the reaching branches stretch
A millimeter more towards heaven,
The bole expand ever so slightly
And push roots into the firm
Foundation, lucky to be leafless:
Deciduous reminder to let it go.

The Lucky Sad

"Blessed are those who mourn"

Flash floods of tears, torrents of them,
Erode cruel canyons, exposing
Long forgotten strata of life
Laid down in the peaceful decades:
A badlands beauty. The same sun
That decorates each day with colors
From arroyos and mesas, also shows
Every old scar and cut of lament.
Weeping washes the wounds clean
And leaves them to heal, which always
Takes an age or two. No pain
Is ugly in past tense. Under
The Mercy every hurt is a fossil
Link in the great chain of becoming.
Pick and shovel prayers often
Turn them up in valleys of death.

The Lucky Meek

"Blessed are the meek"

Moses, by turns raging and afraid,
Was meek under the thunderhead whiteness,
The glorious opacity of cloudy pillar.
Each cloud is meek, buffeted by winds
It changes shape but never loses
Being: not quite liquid, hardly
Solid, *in medias res*, like me.
Yielding to the gusting spirit
All become what ministering angels
Command: sign, promise, portent.
Vigorous in image and color, oh, colors
Of earth pigments mixed with sun
Make hues that raise praises at dusk,
At dawn, collect storms, release
Rain, filter sun in arranged
And weather measured shadows. Sunpatches.

The Lucky Hungry

"Blessed are those who hunger and thirst after righteousness"

Unfeathered unbelief would fall
Through the layered fullness of thermal
Updrafts like a rock; this red-tailed
Hawk drifts and slides, unhurried
Though hungry, lazily scornful
Of easy meals off carrion junkfood,
Expertly waiting elusive provisioned
Prey: a visible emptiness
Above an invisible plenitude.
The sun paints the Japanese
Fantail copper, etching
Feathers against the big sky
To my eye's delight, and blesses
The better-sighted bird with a shaft
Of light that targets a rattler
In a Genesis-destined death.

The Lucky Merciful

"Blessed are the merciful"

A billion years of pummeling surf,
Shipwrecking seachanges and Jonah storms
Made ungiving, unforgiving granite
Into this analgesic beach:
Washed by sea-swell rhythms of mercy,
Merciful relief from city
Concrete. Uncondemned, discalceate,
I'm ankle deep in Assateague sands,
Awake to rich designs of compassion
Patterned in the pillowing dunes.
Sandpipers and gulls in skittering,
Precise formation devoutly attend
My salt and holy solitude,
Then feed and fly along the moving,
Imprecise ebb- and rip-tide
Border dividing care from death.

The Lucky Pure

"Blessed are the pure in heart"

Austere country, this, scrubbed
By spring's ravaging avalanche.
Talus slope and Appekunny
Mudstone make a meadow where
High-country beargrass gathers light
From lichen, rock, and icy tarn,
Changing sun's lethal rays
To food for grizzlies, drink for bees —
Heart-pure creatures living blessed
Under the shining of God's face.
Yet, like us the far-fallen,
Neither can they look on the face
And live. Every blossom's a breast
Holding eventual sight for all blind and
Groping newborn: we touch our way
Through these splendors to the glory.

The Lucky Peacemakers

"Blessed are the peacemakers"

Huge cloud fists assault
The blue exposed bare midriff of sky:
The firmament doubles up in pain,
Lightnings rip and thunders shout;
Mother nature's children quarrel.
And then, as suddenly as it began,
It's over. Noah's heirs, perceptions
Cleansed, look out on a disarmed world
At ease and ozone fragrant. Still waters.
What barometric shift
Rearranged these ferocities
Into a peace-pulsating rainbow
Sign? My enemy turns his other
Cheek; I drop my guard. A mirror
Lake reflects the filtered colors;
Breeze-stirred pine trees quietly sing.

The Lucky Persecuted

"Blessed are those who are persecuted"

Unfriendly waters do a friendly
Thing: curses, cataract-hurled
Stones, make the rough places
Smooth; a rushing whitewater stream
Of blasphemies hate-launched,
Then caught by the sun, sprays rainbow
Arcs across the Youghiogheny.
Savaged by the river's impersonal
Attack the land is deepened to bedrock.
Wise passivities are learned
In quiet, craggy occasional pools
That chasten the wild waters to stillness,
And hold them under hemlock green
For birds and deer to bathe and drink
In peace — persecution's gift:
The hard-won, blessed letting be.

II. The Rustling Grass

In the rustling grass
I hear him pass;
He speaks to me everywhere.

MALTBIE BABCOCK

Cradle

She gave birth to her first-born son
And wrapped him in swaddling clothes,
And laid him in a manger.

LUKE 2:7

For us who have only known approximate fathers
And mothers manqué, this child is a surprise:
A sudden coming true of all we hoped
Might happen. Hoarded hopes fed by prophecies,

    Old sermons and song fragments now cry
    Coo and gurgle in the cradle, a babbling
    Proto-language which as soon as it gets
    A tongue (and we, of course, grow open ears)

Will say the big nouns: joy, glory, peace;
And live the best verbs: love, forgive, save.
Along with the swaddling clothes the words are washed

    Of every soiling sentiment, scrubbed clean
    Of all failed promises, then hung in the world's
    Backyard dazzling white, billowing gospel.

Dream

. . . an angel of the Lord appeared to him in a dream

MATTHEW 1:20

Amiably conversant with virtue and evil,
The righteousness of Joseph and wickedness
Of Herod, I'm ever and always a stranger to grace.
I need this annual angel visitation

    — sudden dive by dream to reality —
    To know the virgin conceives and God is with us.
    The dream powers its way through winter weather
    And gives me vision to see the Jesus gift.

Light from the dream lasts a year. Impervious
To equinox and solstice it makes twelve months
Of daylight by which I see the crèche where my

    Redeemer lives. Archetypes of praise take shape
    Deep in my spirit. As autumn wanes I count
    The days 'til I will have the dream again.

Tree

There shall come forth a shoot from the stump of Jesse,
And a branch shall grow out of his roots.

ISAIAH 11:1

Jesse's roots, composted with carcasses
Of dove and lamb, parchments of ox and goat,
Centuries of dried up prayers and bloody
Sacrifice, now bear me gospel fruit.

   David's branch fed on kosher soil
   Blossoms a messianic flower, and then
   Ripens into a kingdom crop, conserving
   The fragrance and warmth of spring for winter use.

Holy Spirit, shake our family tree;
Release your ripened fruit to our outstretched arms.

   I'd like to see my children sink their teeth
   Into promised land pomegranates

And Canaan grapes, bushel gifts of God,
While I skip a grace rope to a Christ tune.

Present

For to us a child is born, to us a son is given . . . and his name will be called Wonderful, Counselor, Mighty God, Everlasting Father, Prince of peace.

ISAIAH 9:6

Half-sick with excitement and under garish lights
I do it again, year after year after year
I can't wait to plunder the boxes, then show
And tell my friends: Look what I got!

    I rip the tissues from every gift but find
    That all the labels lied. Stones.
    And my heart a stone. "Dead in trespasses
    And sin." The lights go out. Later my eyes,

Accustomed to the dark, see wrapped
In Christ-foil and ribboned in Spirit-colors

    The multi-named messiah, love labels
    On a faith shape, every name a promise

And every promise a present, made and named
All in the same breath. I accept.

Kiss

Steadfast love and faithfulness will meet;
Righteousness and peace will kiss each other.

PSALM 85:10

Stray affections, following their noses,
Get me into all kinds of trouble, from trampling
Beds of roses to scattering unbagged garbage.
And then the trails grow cold. It is "winter

    All the time and Christmas never comes,"
    'til pulled on tip-toe to get it full on the lips
    Under the psalmic mistletoe I'm kissed.
    Peace compressed into lips that make a sign

Of love slowly releases eternity
Into time: I'm touched into joy.

    Always awkward with heavenly intimacies
    In public places, I shuffle and blush and contribute,

Despite myself, brightness to the night
And warmth to the winter. The world's a lover's lane.

Pain

... and a sword will pierce through your own soul also that thoughts out of many hearts may be revealed.

LUKE 2:35

The bawling of babies, always in a way
Inappropriate — why should the loved and innocent
Greet existence with wails? — is proof that not all
Is well. Dreams and deliveries never quite mesh.

    Deep hungers go unsatisfied, deep hurts
    Unhealed. The natural and gay are torn
    By ugly grimace and curse. A wound appears
    In the place of ecstasy. Birth is bloody.

All pain's a prelude: to symphony, to sweetness.
"The pearl began as a pain in the oyster's stomach."

    Dogwood, recycled from cradle to cross, enters
    The market again as a yoke for easing burdens.

Each sword-opened side is the matrix for God
To come again through travail for joy.

Dance

. . . when the voice of your greeting came to my ears the babe in my womb leaped for joy.

LUKE 1:44

Another's heart lays down the beat that puts
Me in motion, in perichoresis, steps
Learned in the womb before the world's foundation.
It never misses a beat: praise pulses.

    Leaping towards the light, I'm dancing in
    The dark, touching now the belly of blessing,
    Now the aching side, ready for birth,
    For naming and living love's mystery out in the open.

The nearly dead and the barely alive pick up
The chthonic rhythms in their unused muscles

    And gaily cartwheel three hallelujahs.
    But not all: "those who are deaf always despise

Those who dance." That doesn't stop the dance. Unapplauded,
All waiting for light leap at the voice of greeting.

Star

I see him, but not now, I behold him, but not nigh:
A star shall come forth out of Jacob . . .

NUMBERS 24:17

No star is visible except at night,
Until the sun goes down, no accurate north.
Day's brightness hides what darkness shows to sight,
The hour I go to sleep the bear strides forth.

    I open my eyes to the cursed but requisite dark,
    The black sink that drains my cistern dry,
    And see, not nigh, not now, the heavenly mark
    Exploding in the quasar-messaged sky.

Out of the dark, behind my back, a sun
Launched light-years ago completes its run.

    The undeciphered skies of myth and story
    Now narrate the cadenced runes of glory.

Lost pilots wait for night to plot their flight,
Just so diurnal pilgrims praise the midnight.

Time

When the time had fully come, God sent forth his Son, born of a woman, born under the law, to redeem those who were under the law, that we might receive adoption . . .

GALATIANS 4:4-5

Half, or more than half, my life is spent
In waiting: waiting for the day to come
When dawn spills laughter's animated sun
Across the rim of God into my tent.

In my other clock sin I put off
Until I'm ready, which I never seem
To be, the seized day, the kingdom dream
Come true. My head has been too long in the trough.

Keeping a steady messianic rhythm,
Ocean tides and woman's blood fathom

The deep that calls to deep and bring to birth
The seeded years and grace this wintered earth.

Measured by the metronomic moon,
Nothing keeps time better than a womb.

Candle

The people who walked in darkness
    have seen a great light; those who dwelt
In a land of deep darkness,
    on them has light shined.

ISAIAH 9:2

Uncandled menorahs and oiless lamps abandoned
By foolish virgins too much in a hurry to wait
And tend the light are clues to the failed watch,
The missed arrival, the midnight might-have-been.

   Wick and beeswax make a guttering protest,
   Fragile, defiant flame against demonic
   Terrors that gust invisible and nameless
   Out of galactic ungodded emptiness.

Then deep in the blackness fires nursed by wise
Believers surprise with shining all groping derelicts
Bruised and stumbling in a world benighted.

   A sudden blazing backlights each head with a nimbus.
   Shafts of storm-filtered sun search and destroy
   The Stygian desolation: I see I see.

Offertory

May the kings of Tarshish and the isles render him tribute,
may the kings of Sheba and Seba bring gifts.
Long may he live, may gold of Sheba be given to him!

PSALM 72:10, 15

Brought up in a world where there's no free lunch
And trained to use presents for barter, I'm spending
The rest of my life receiving this gift with no
Strings attached, but not doing too well.

    Three bathrobed wise men with six or seven
    Inches of jeans and sneakers showing, kneel
    Offering gifts that symbolize the gifts
    That none of us are ready yet to give.

A few of us stay behind, blow out the candles,
Sweep up the straw and put the crèche in storage.

    We open the door into the world's night
    And find we've played ourselves into a better

Performance. We leave with our left-over change
Changed at the offertory into kingdom gold.

War

And the dragon stood before the woman
who was about to bear a child
that he might devour her child.
. . . Now war arose in heaven   REVELATION 12:4, 7

This birth's a signal for war. Lovers fight,
Friends fall out, merry toasts from flagons
Of punch are swallowed in the maw of dragons.
Will mother and baby survive this devil night?

    I've done my share of fighting in the traffic:
    Kitchen quarrels, playgound fisticuffs;
    Every cherub choir has its toughs.
    And then one day I learned the fight was cosmic.

Truce. I lay down arms, my arms fill up
With gifts — wild and tame, real and stuffed

    Lions, lambs play, oxen low,
    This infant fathers festive force. One crow

Croaks defiance into the shalom whiteness,
Empty satanic bluster against the brightness.

Choir

Glory to God in the highest and on earth
Peace with whom he is pleased.

LUKE 2:14

Untuned, I'm flat on my feet, sharp with my tongue,
A walking talking discord, out of sorts,
My heart murmurs are entered in lab reports.
The noise between my ears cannot be sung.

Ill-pleased, I join a line of hard-to-please people
Who want to exchange their lumpy bourgeois souls
For a keen Greek mind with a strong Roman nose,
Then find ourselves, surprised, at the edge of a stable.

Caroling angels and a well-pleased God
Join a choir of cow and sheep and dog

At this barnyard border between wish and gift.
I glimpse the just-formed flesh, now mine. They lift

Praise voices and sing twelve tones
Of pleasure into my muscles, into my bones.

Greetings

Hail, O favored one, the Lord is with you!

LUKE 1:28

My mail carrier driving his stubby white
Truck, trimmed in blue and red, wingless
But wheeled, commissioned by the civil service,
Delivers the Gospel every Advent.

This Gabriel, uniformed in gabardine,
Unsmiling descendent of his dazzling original,
Under the burden of greetings is stoical
But prompt: annunciations at ten each morning.

One or two or three a day at first;
By the second week momentum's up,
My mailbox stuffed, each card stamped

With the glory at a cost of only twenty-two cents,
Bringing the news that God is here with us,
First class, personally hand addressed.

Feast

He who is mighty has done great things for me . . .
He has filled the hungry with good things.

LUKE 1:49, 53

The milk full breasts brim blessings and quiet
This child in fullness, past pain: El Shaddai
Has done great things for me. Earth nurses
Heaven on the slopes of the Grand Tetons.

> Grown up, he gave breakfasts, broke bread,
> Itinerant host at feasts with his friends.
> His milkfed bones were buried unbroken
> Deep in the Arimathean's tomb.

The world has worked up an appetite
And comes on the run to the table he set:
Strong meat, full-bodied wine.

> Wassailing with my friends in the winter
> Mountains, I'm back for seconds as often
> As every week: drink long! drink up!

Stamp

He reflects the glory of God
And bears the very stamp of his nature.

HEBREWS 1:3

I tear along the perforated edge,
Tongue the mucilage, then press the image
Across the enveloped message: it flies by magic
Carpet across the mountains and over the seas

    Into all the world, a postmarked
    Prophecy validating love
    Come down from heaven, delivered posthaste
    To every waiting mailbox.

Be a stamp collector: notice, gather,
Post the thin paper angels streaming
Glory into Ezekiel's book of life.

    Philatelic witnesses display
    Caesar at piece-work, stamping the Nature into
    Amnesiac lives, canceling our wordless waiting.

Womb

And behold you will conceive in your womb . . .
The Holy Spirit will come upon you
And the power of the Most High will overshadow you.

LUKE 1:31, 35

Buy a packaged God, and then another
And another and another — a god
For every godless friend, a one-size-fits-all
God certified good without bother of love.

   Vacuumed wombs are ripe for stuffing at market
   Discounts: capture the season's spirit at bargain
   Prices, buy a manufactured joy
   Guaranteed not to surprise with squall or mess.

But when the wind gusts in your belly, the storm
Spirit, holy and heavenly, begins to swell
You hugely pregnant, drop the packages,

   Feel the kicking, dancing God within
   And let Him grow the Christ-shape in you.
   Phylogeny recapitulates ontogeny.

Question

How can this be, since I have no husband?

LUKE 1:34

The impossible possibility (or is it
The possible impossibility?) throws a question
Mark across my life. Am I engaged to
Death or life? Am I a womb?

    Silently my sex secretes fluids.
    My body fills with a pool of questions:
    Will the water drown or baptize?
    Am I Dead Sea or Jordan River?

Bargaining with God for improved death
Benefits (I thought that's what you did
With God) I'm stopped in my tracks.

    Do I want mystery within me?
    Will this life cost my life?
    Am I ready to make love with my life?

Dawn

The day shall dawn upon us from on high
To give light to those who sit in darkness.

Tearful, we shuffled through the fallen
Leaves of autumn, going over the losses,
Counting the dead, remembering the old
Good times, knowing they were gone for good.

   We came to an unmarked door and knocked;
   A voice called, Open. We opened and light
   Rivered across our ice-age silence
   And steel weather, tonguing light

Along the Susquehanna, translating
Our wept-over dead into morning light

   Down the Monongahela, raising
   Our sacrificed loves into dawn gifts and

Up the Allegheny, rainbowing
Our faithful friends into arcs of light.

Egypt

Rise, take the child and his mother,
  And flee to Egypt.   MATTHEW 2:13

The angel word to leave was clear enough but
It couldn't have been easy — all those months
In rented rooms. We've, at least, not found it
So. Egypt was safe but it wasn't home.

  How many ruined altars did you find
  Along the way, rebuild and offer sacrifice?
  A few of Abraham's perhaps? Was there
  Rubble marking Elijah's run for dear life?

And glances of sun-glint off ravens' wings? Promises
Kept in unpromising places. And then the

  All-clear: safe passage back to homeland
  Woods and waters, country of first visions,

Tucked away in the ordinary,
Holy and hidden in village obscurity.

Message

Climb a high mountain, Zion,
*   You've been entrusted with the message!*
Shout, O Jerusalem, at the top of your lungs,
*   You've been entrusted with the message!*
Shout boldly, fearlessly, to Judah's cities,
*   "Look, listen! God is here, now!"*   ISAIAH 40:9

A long climb it was to the top of the mountain,
Thirty-five years all told, counting in detours and
Rest stops. Thirty-five years in the company
Of friends and family, climbing, climbing, climbing.

>   Sundays were blaze marks as we hiked our way
>   Through scree and scrub alder, picking huckleberries,
>   Learning the high country language
>   From journals and letters of pioneer climbers.

The summit was sudden, we caught our breath
As range after range spread out beneath us.

>   Stunned into silence, our voiceless praise
>   Choired with firs and saskatoons,

Every mountain a pulpit and the message out,
"Here! Oh, he's here! Look! Listen!"

Lights

Every gift that's good for you
   Comes out of heaven.
The gifts are rivers of light
   Cascading down from the Father of light.

JAMES 1:17

I showed up with a wish list, hoping
For a gift or two, and walked into
A party lavish with light and gifts,
Light from parents and grandchildren,

   Spouse and children, brothers and sisters,
   Lovers and friends: light from the Father
   Of light — light gifts rivering
   Out of faces and sky and making me

Light of step, light of heart,
The beauty of the Lord pulsating from
These icons of Adam, icons of Eve.

   Light from the East, light from the West,
   Winter light and summer light.
   We love and work and die in light.

Pregnancy

My little children,
  With whom I am again in travail,
Until Christ be formed in you!

GALATIANS 4:19

Pregnant by my parents' prayers,
I'm large with child; I wait, shy
In the mystery, larger inside than outside.
Am I showing? Does anyone notice?

  The dark interior of my life
  Enlarges with light. Proto-lineaments
  Of the Savior take shape. I feel
  The kick of joy, the dance of grace.

Meeting with others, also due,
Arthritic octogenarians and willowy
Virgins, kneeling quiet in sacred

  Shadows, we listen to creation
  Groan, time the pains, and know
  We're about to know as we've been known.

Glory

The Word became flesh and blood,
  And moved into the neighborhood.
We saw the glory with our own eyes,
  The one-of-a-kind glory,
Like Father, like Son,
  Generous inside and out,
True from start to finish   JOHN 1:14

Sixty years ago I was a boy here.
Now driving through the old neighborhood
I find the pasture where we'd played our games
Using dried cow flop to mark goals and bases,

  All macadamized: buttercups
  And dandelions flattened under white
  Stripes; the sweet scent of heifers
  Lost in exhaust fumes. Everything changed.

Yet nothing has changed: sky large as ever,
Foothills working their way up to alpine
Peaks, and one huge Douglas fir,

  Already huge when I was four and under
  Which I first heard the Story — saw the
  Glory. The story is the glory. Shekinah.

Meditation

Mary kept all these things to herself,
Holding them dear, deep within herself.

LUKE 2:19

Messages pile up, not all but some
From angels: by person and post and fax.
Each annunciation pulls me deeper
Into providential but dark-shadowed mystery.

    I'm keeping track of the comings and goings,
    Birth announcements and death notices,
    Cries from the cradle, cries from the cross.
    Births and burials stay about even.

And I'm a womb of meditation,
Each new presence, each fresh absence
Metabolizing into soul song.

    Hold them — Oh, hold them! — each baby,
    Each burial, as the songs and sighs
    Work their way into a Jesus hymn.

Homecoming

Ho, everyone who thirsts,
   Come to the waters;
And you who have no money,
   Come, buy wine and milk
Without money and without price.   ISAIAH 55:1

I come. I've been working my way to this
Since the womb. But leaving is hard,
Emptying my pockets of wallet and passport,
Leaving the bright lights, leaving the sights.

   Pre-advent tamaracks show the way,
   Exploding from green to gold, bursting
   Into flares marking the way home,
   Laying down, needle by needle, gold carpet.

I grew up on conifers,
Evergreen fir and pine and spruce.
Tamaracks are an annual surprise,

   Opening the woods to winter light,
   Invitation to a less that is more.
   I loosen my grip, slow my pace, coming home.

Story

I'm here to announce a great
*   And joyful event that is meant for everybody worldwide:*
A Savior has just been born in David's town,
*   A Savior who is Messiah and Master.*

LUKE 2:10-11

The virgin and angel got an early start
On us: in Alabama and Montana
We got the story that forms the world
Into our muscles and synapses and bones.

   We had our babies and buried our parents;
   The Story took our stories into itself;
   We watched the stories swell with miracle and meaning,
   As cradle and cross gave plot. Predawn

We climb our neighborhood Nebo and watch
The sun bring light to mountain waters
Rivering and pooling in the valley below us,

   And to the towns and forests and roads:
   Geography of our salvation. A story
   Complete; a story not yet complete.

Quiet

In returning and rest you shall be saved,
In quietness and trust shall be your strength.

ISAIAH 30:15

Our latest guest, a common loon,
Arrived this winter unannounced
And bringing gifts — guests do that,
Bring gifts — filling heart and home

    With beauty: wild, elusive, sleek,
    Low in the water, this contemplative
    Loon is an icon for living present
    But detached. I rarely see him fly

But he can fly. This loon dives, dives
Long and deep. No mere surface
Bird, he goes for the depths. When he dives

    I think he prays, searching deep waters
    For what keeps him and us alive,
    Grace and quiet, buoyant with Presence.

Terror

Herod . . . flew into a rage. He commanded the murder
Of every little boy two years old and under
Who lived in Bethlehem and its surrounding hills.   MATTHEW 2:16

If the foundations are destroyed
What can the righteous do?   PSALM 11:3

The Holy Day is purged, at least for this year,
Of silliness, all trees stripped of tinsel.
Christ's cradle soaked in blood,
Shepherds and Wise Men choked with smoke.

But even while Herod grabs the headlines,
Leviathan spews fire, and Behemoth's on the loose,
This Child we worship is alive in the rubble.
"And if the foundations are destroyed . . . ?"

Last week I walked along Ole Creek
Past the giant cottonwood, lightning-struck
In that wild, autumn storm — riven

But upright still on hidden roots.
"The road up and the road down are the same road."
Evil is the palindrome of live.

Snow

He spreads snow like white fleece,
  He scatters frost like ashes,
He broadcasts hail like birdseed —
  Who can survive his winter?
Then he gives the command and it all melts;
  He breathes on winter — suddenly it's spring.

PSALM 147:16-18

Losing steam, another year
Cools down, loosens its grip on aspen
And larch, drops leaves and needles,
Bids them return, earth to earth.

  And now the gift of drifting snow,
  Wind-sculpted beauty. Cold comfort
  (not all His gifts are cozy) invites
  Entrance into a season of austere

Emptiness: "nothing in my hand
I bring." Septuagenarian joints
Stiffen in snow-clad cold. Chilled

  In the expiring sun, we squint
  Through the Narrow Gate: the candle
  Flames; we lift our glasses, *l'chaim,* "to Life!"

Ancestors

. . . the genealogy of Jesus Christ . . .
Amminadab begat Nashan . . .
Boaz begat Obed by Ruth . . .
Jehoshaphat begat Joram . . .

MATTHEW 1:1, 4-5, 8

We went looking for ancestors in Norway
And Sweden, saw some features in bodies and faces
Familiar from childhood, heard the original music
Of the language that had lost its lilt in America.

But no names: no cousins, no uncles, no aunts.
All the begats eroded in the Jotenheimen
Mountains where we hiked, flanked by
Prehistoric glaciers, looking for clues.

We've done some begetting ourselves in the new
Country — a daughter and two sons for a start.
The lineage continues. We look for signs

That the old genes are still at work:
An Amminadab nose here, Ruth's high cheek bones,
There Jehoshaphat's chin — and Jesus?

Silence

. . . yet he opened not his mouth.

ISAIAH 53:7

The temptation is always to say too much,
Compensate for His non-saying
With verbal tinsel and bauble tunes.
Unnerved by the dimming of angel glory,

    Fading echoes of exuberant hosannas,
    We dazzle with evangelical smiles,
    Amplify earnestness to deafen doubt,
    Then miss the pre-dawn silence-swaddled virgin

Birth. Quiet is the only adequate
Womb thick enough to shut out
The devil's noise, protect a life

    Of listening. Silence and only silence is
    Congenial humus for this seed that will burst
    In resurrection through death's mute crust.

Beauty

He had no form or comeliness
That we should look at him,
And no beauty that we should desire him.

A whiff. A beagle for beauty I sniffed
Monet's haystacks, van Gogh's sunflowers,
Devoutly meditated Marilyn's breasts,
Watched kingfishers — lost the scent.

    Kiss the leper's wound: taste honey.
    Touch the blind eye: learn Braille.
    Keep vigil at the cradle: change diapers.
    Drink tears from the chalice: live eucharist.

Happened on found things, found in gutters,
Found on a cross, found under a stone,

    Heard in the rustling grass, heard in
    A tongue stammering *sabachthani.*

Found when I wasn't looking, heard
When I wasn't listening. Found beauty.

Hospitality

. . . no room for them in the inn.

LUKE 2:7

Practice hospitality ungrudgingly.

1 PETER 4:9

Benedict taught us well: Receive
Each guest as Christ. The bell rings, the door
Opens. Some unexpected, and some, yes,
Unwelcome. Our guest book spills out photos.

 Christ abused, Christ the fool,
 Christ sullen, Christ laughing,
 Christ angry, Christ envious,
 Christ bewildered, Christ on crutches.

Like Gospel writers of old we pray
And reminisce over left-behind guest signs —
A bra, a sock, a scribbled thank you —

 And let them grow into stories. Sometimes
 It takes an unhurried while. Then,
 There it is: absences become Presence. Resurrection.

Uncle Ernie

A tree from the forest is cut down
. . . men deck it with silver and gold.

JEREMIAH 10:3-4

My uncle Ernie didn't believe in God.
At least that's what he said. But he always
Went to church on Christmas. Which I thought
Seriously compromised his atheism. It was

    Nineteen thirty-seven, the year we didn't
    Have a tree. He came to dinner, looked
    Around and roared, "Evie" (that's my mother)
    "Where's the tree? You can't have Christmas

Without a tree!" "No tree this year, brother.
Just Jesus." She quoted Jeremiah on the tree
Cut down and decked with baubles and tinsel. Stunned

    By her impiety he muttered through a mouth full
    Of lutefisk "damn, damn, damn, damn"
    All through dinner. Next year the tree was back.

Altar

Another angel with a golden censer came
  and stood at the altar; he was given a great
Quantity of incense to offer with the prayers
  of all the saints on the golden altar . . . then
The angel took the censer . . . from the altar
  and threw it on the earth
And there were peals of thunder.   REVELATION 8:3-5

Yesterday on a Sabbath walk
We climbed our local Mt. Pisgah to view
"The whole land" that is now our promised land
Home, we passed the ancient stump

  Of a Douglas fir my mother, now dead,
  Often used as an altar on prayer walks (I once
  Counted two hundred and twenty rings).
  We carried a load of pain. We rested,

Climbed to the summit, placed the gut-wrenching
Pain-evoked prayers on the golden mountain

  Altar, surveyed the salvation country,
  Then hurled the prayers incensed with tears

For all innocent and betrayed souls on earth,
Heaved them — and listened for peals of thunder.

Yes and Amen and Jesus

Whatever God has promised
   gets stamped with the Yes of Jesus.
In him, this is what we preach and pray,
   the great Amen, God's Yes and our Yes together,
Gloriously evident. God affirms us,
   making us a sure thing in Christ,
Putting his Yes within us.   2 CORINTHIANS 1:20-22

We celebrate a lifetime — going on
Eight decades now of Yes
And Amen. Not all green eggs and ham,
But mostly Yes and Amen and Jesus.

   Three children, six grandchildren,
   Faithful friends, honored work,
   Good words, requited love,
   Holy people, sacred ground.

Years ago we placed a seven-ton
Standing stone, a silent weighty
Witness like the bronze age standing stones

   At Gezer, to mark this place, evidence
   Of things not seen, as we daily make our way
   Through this Yes and Amen and Jesus world.

Green

They still bring forth fruit in old age,
they are ever full of sap and green.

PSALM 92:14

A poet we respected when we
Were young (we read him on our honeymoon)
Advised "Do not go gentle into
That good night." No. We *want* to go

    Gentle, embrace the Sabbath rest.
    New country for us: valleys
    To stroll through instead of mountains
    To climb. Liturgical naps after lunch.

"Fruit in old age?" "Sap and green?"
Less adrenalin, more love.
Words swell like buds about

    To burst into leaf while the gentled
    Lake laps against driftwood, green
    On gray, and a loon bugles taps.

Friends

I have called you friends.

JESUS (JOHN 15:15)

Skating on thin ice had always
Been my forte, cursive figure
Eights my speciality. I'd never
Stubbed my toe, never eaten

    Crow, four-leaf clovers lined
    My path with Irish luck. An untroubled
    Life 'til barbarians stormed the gates
    Spewing hate in Jesus' name.

Then voices, but these melodic with beauty,
Rose from the street through my open window,
Children singing *Amigos de Christo,*

    We're friends of the Lord, Amigos
    De Christo, we're friends of the Lord.
    What a friend we have in Jesus.

III. Smooth Stones
(Occasional Poems)

Smooth Stones

David ... chose five smooth stones
  From the brook.

1 SAMUEL 17:40

Odd shaped pebbles roll
And tumble 'round the Rock which
Smooths them into five smooth
Stones
One of which will
Kill a giant.

A Prayer of Blessing for Trygve the New
(Trygve David Johnson, Jr. Born August 11, 2009)

Bless, God, Trygve the New with metaphors
    Accurate and adequate:

An arrow in his father's quiver,
    An olive shoot 'round his mother's table,

Firstborn, first fruits of his parents' vigor,
    A haven for ships, a lion's whelp,

A fruitful bough, a fruitful bough by a spring,
    His branches run over the wall,

His name engraved on the palms of God's hands,
    His feet beautiful upon the mountains.

    Amen.

Assateague Island

All thy waves and billows
Have gone over me.   PSALM 42:7

A double-crested c ormorant,
    Brobdingnagian duck, black
On green, cushioned by six or seven
    Inches of air above the killing
Billows, wings a swift passage
    Through the wet wave troughs.

Beneath the bird water gathers and crests
    In curved mandalas, crashes in mantra
Chants, then slides down the strand
    Into the deep where ocean spray
Is recollected in the great
    Salt, billow-making womb.

Effortless elegance!
    Holy wildness!

We walked nine miles of ocean beach
    Yesterday and let the ocean
Rhythms — pulse-setting waves and tide-making
    Moon — get inside us. Slowed
By this ancient pacemaker
    Our hearts thirsted. We drank God.

Lazarus in Spring

Burst of bloodroot, blush
Of bloom from under the burlap-
Textured shroud of matted
Oak leaves and pine needles,
Is the unsurprised surprise
When Lazarus comes forth.

Beware the Dogs *(Cave Canem)*

PHILIPPIANS 3:2

God spelled backwards is tame,
Companion for long walks,
Fireside friend at night.

I get a tail-wagging welcome
Every time I retreat
From the too-rough world.

Past challenge, I'm almighty;
Adored and obeyed, cozy
And enthroned on a footstool.

Prayer Time

I've never had an answered
Prayer
Or unanswered.

There's a clearing
Away or a darkening over,
A quickened pulse or
Slowed step, not

Getting but
Getting in on
God.

    Being there.

Intercessory Prayer

Praying mantis
Pray for me.

I need your insect
Intercession.

I've never heard
You make a sound,

Still I'd like
Your still small voice

To pray for me.

Aaron's Beard

... running down the beard,
upon the beard of Aaron ...

PSALM 133:2

Aaronic blessings
Run down my red beard
Refracting sun warmth
In oil ooze
   loosening
Ironic curses
Flecks of stubborn rust
Corrosive unbelief
Cynic stuff.

Lent

The pale winter sun slants
Cool warmth
Across my iced mind
And promises a future thaw.

Four horses thunder through the storm
Of sin's hot hail
And splash apocalyptic colors
On my white-washed sepulcher.

Baptismal rains release blossom-
Bursting shrubs and trees
From a cemetery winter
Into a resurrection spring.

Charismatic colors claim the earth.
Every fruit branch swings a censer
Through the air
Floating smells of praise.

Hell

Flabby toothless minds grin
And show the devil's double chin
Set on a neck of crepuscular sin.

Aquarian ghosts wrapped in sables
Wander stoned through eastern stables
And renovate discarded fables.

Amoebic water in inky pools
Rusts a garbage heap of tools
And poisons throats of thirsty fools.

Ascension

Space is sanctified today
As time will be next week. Bronze
Age Bethels, Shilohs, Gilgals
Slip their geographic chains,
Pop up on every continent
And most states. Rand McNally
Maps locate gospel witnesses
Marked with red dots or black
Circles, depending on the number
Of saints and sinners who have a house
Or room there. Holy sites and lands
Define the landscape since Jesus' ascent.

Shalom

Strong God of Jacob, dear Lord of hosts,
    God of the fathers, Lord of the lost,
Dissolve our terrors, quiet our fears:
    Whisper your kind Shalom.

All laws are broken, all peace disturbed,
    Rumors of wars unsettle our hearts,
Our loves are ruined, our hopes decayed:
    Love us and speak Shalom.

Rough ocean waters drown us in doubt,
    Volcanic thunders shake our repose,
Sinai is shattered, Galilee churned:
    Firm our faith with Shalom.

Plunge us in Jordan's baptismal stream,
    Dig us a deep Samaritan well,
Waters to wash the guilt from our land:
    Cleanse us and sing Shalom.

Great God of refuge, near God of help,
    Wreck the armadas of sin and death,
Be quick in mercy, be swift in love,
    Save us and make Shalom.

Light on Light

Pin that butterfly to a stick,
Label its ambiguity.
Impale on thin steel the filigreed beauty,
Make the world safe for law and order.

Transfix the lepidopteral dances
So I can view them at my leisure.
Mount them on a varnished board,
A frieze to decorate my boredom.

Or maybe I could learn to loose
My spirit to flutter with similar wings,
And light on light petals long enough
To inhale blues and touch greens.

Maranatha

Our Lord, Come!
Maranatha

1 CORINTHIANS 16:22

Christ, come quickly, judge my thoughts,
Show my sin, bare my pride,
Separate my sheep and goats.
 Now, Lord, Maranatha.

Christ, come quickly, tame my will,
Shape my hopes, save my dreams,
Set me high on Zion's hill.
 Today, Lord, Maranatha.

Christ, come quickly, redeem my lust,
Purge my loves, sift my heart,
Resurrect this Adam's dust.
 Soon, Lord, Maranatha.

Christ, come quickly, open the door,
Show us heaven's rainbow throne,
Reveal the Lamb that we adore.
 At once, Lord, Maranatha.

Christ, come quickly, make new pastures
For ox and eagle, lion and man,
Bless the four and living creatures.
    At dawn, Lord, Maranatha.

Christ, come quickly, invite this pauper,
Break the bread and pour the wine,
Begin the glorious marriage supper.
    It's midnight, Maranatha.

Birdwatching

Merganser
Dive, merganser, deep, deep:
Eat your fill of minnows and weeds.
Surface glistening, your rust-red head
Radiant under the big sky.
Your lithe grace is daily bread,
Breakfast at matins,
Supper at vespers.
Buoyant on the world's waters,
With frequent descents for food and
Occasional flights for safety,
Easily afloat on
The sun-gathering, food-yielding blue waters.

Nuthatch
Quack like a duck, your wedge of feathers
Descending, foraging for bugs.
Wake me, your sleeping friend,
Set me upright, straight
As a tamarack, needled and green,
Reaching for the sky.

Kingfisher
Plummet the blue, kingfisher;
Pierce the green, spear
Your daily fish, then
Rattle your rusty gate clatter
Across the acoustic, cat's paw surface.
Perch solemn in comic dignity,
Your cumberbund strapped
Belly resplendent in rust and blue and white
Mirrored in the lake.
I love receiving your greetings from Maryland rivers
And Montana ponderosas and glinting
Off the lead crystal mug my daughter
Made and gave me,
First love from the company
Of Adam's flying things,
Reversed icon of my Fisher King.

Let Not Man Put Asunder

Committed by command and habit to fidelity
I'm snug in the double bed and board of marriage.

    Spontaneity's built-in
    To the covenantal dance,
    Everyday routines arranged
    In the rhythms of the manse.

This unlikely fissiparous alliance
Embraces and releases daily surprises.

    The ego strength we'd carefully hoarded
    In certain safe-deposit boxes
    We've now dispersed, unlamented
    In dozens of delicate paradoxes.

A thousand domestic intimacies are straw
For making bricks resistant to erosion:

    With such uncomely stuff we've built
    Our lives on ordinary sod
    And grow, finally, old. My love is
    Not a goddess nor am I a god.

Asunder is the one unpronounceable word in the world
Of the wed, one flesh the mortal miracle.

What started out quite tentatively
With clumsy scrawls in a billet-doux
Has now become the intricacy
Of bold marriage's pas de deux.

Ballad to the Fisher King

Pete and Andy and Jack and Jim
    Sailed in sturdy ships.
They were fishermen who plowed the sea
    While curses flowed from their lips.

    Heigh ho to the Fisher King, Heigh ho
    Heigh ho to the Fisher Christ.

The world for them was stuff to grab,
    The sea a chest to plunder;
Creation was a vacant lot
    And not a place for wonder.

    Heigh ho to the Fisher King, Heigh ho
    Heigh ho to the Fisher Christ.

They caulked their ships with sticky pitch,
    Were quick at mending a sail.
They swore and sang old chantey tunes
    And drank from a common grail.

    Heigh ho to the Fisher King, Heigh ho
    Heigh ho to the Fisher Christ.

But the fight though hard was joyful and free
    And they sang good songs of blessing.
They helped and healed and loved and prayed
    And seldom missed the fishing.

    Heigh ho to the Fisher King, Heigh ho
    Heigh ho to the Fisher Christ.

Now the fish is a sign of the saving Christ
And a sign of the men he's for,
And a fish is a line you can scratch on the sand
And a meal to feed the poor.

    Heigh ho to the Fisher King, Heigh ho
    Heigh ho to the Fisher Christ.

A Cave of Marriage

These shadows have come in on us
A few times now. More than once
We've felt the darkness, wondered
How deep it would penetrate
Before the candle flame caught,
Held and pushed it back,
Lighting and warming the cave
Where love is born and our loves
Recover in the wintry night.

All year long lovers and would-be
Lovers crowd in. And we've loved
Them, loved them generously, blessing
Them with our love. But tonight
We need to tend our own love,
Light our own candles, huddle
Awhile in a cave of marriage.

We leave the many for the one,
The Thou we each know in the other,
God-love in the beloved.
Maybe we won't go out again.
We have so many stories of love to

Tell, and love songs to sing, and candles
To light — filling this cave with
Opened gifts of each other
And in the shadows, Another.

Sermons from Figs

Without fail the fig is there
Each Sunday morning along with
Scrambled eggs and a toasted bagel.

"To make sure there's biblical
Content in your sermon," she says.
How many years have I been eating

These figs? Dried figs with lineage
To family trees in Eden and
Jerusalem? How many thousands

Of seeds carried in their fig-leather pouches
Have taken root in my stomach?
Did they find there a trodden path,

Or gravel, or shallow dirt, or
Good soil? How many fig tree sermons

Has her love planted,
Has her love pruned and grown?

The New Math

Teach us to number our days
  That we may get a heart of wisdom.

PSALM 90:12

Construct a calendar of grace,
Genesis days and moon-marked months.

  Make a Christian year: add
  Blessings, subtract sins, divide

Sorrow, multiply love —
An arithmetic to confound the devil.

Stations of the Cross

We sat on the church pew that Saturday
Night, praying the stations of the cross.
Fourteen places of pain, pain
Prayed and prayed and prayed.
Our voices antiphonal as we listened
Then spoke, then listened, then
Spoke, praying in sound and silence,
While He prayed in and for us, the pain
Prayed and praying.

On Sunday night the pain was in your eyes,
Your face a station of the cross. And I
Helpless before the pain, dumbly facing
The pain I caused. Black diagonals slanted
Off your cheekbones, furrowing tears.
The love I thought so pure caused
This pain. And you
Became — Christ to me.

The empty woods are a tomb
For burial: bare
Oaks and fog-misted
Hemlocks, kinglets here and there

Embroider the silence
With scarlet-silk sounds.
We enter our Monday
Sabbath. The silence strips us
Piece by piece of guilt
And pride and shame.
By noon we're empty and bare
As the woods, washed
For burial. How long 'til
Dogwoods clothe our nakedness,
Warblers sing our resurrection?

Sabbath Prayers

Five deer startled but still, a summer of oak leaves,
Burnished copper under their hooves

    Holy.

Pileated woodpecker, dwarf descendent of
The pterodactyl, flourishes a winged welcome

    Holy.

Elijah's mantle on our shoulders,
Warm in sweats and down slippers

    Holy.

Three cups of coffee and the fragrance
Of toasted Tassahara bread

    Holy.

Zen in bed,
One flesh

Holy.

A day of winter rain, softly percussive,
Lays down the rhythm for the forest chamber
Orchestra's rendition of Sabbath prayers

Holy.

Chalice of red Cana wine,
Cabernet sauvignon

Holy.

Slow healing wounds
Under the shadow of the full
Moon-brightened cross

Holy.

A wild dawn wind shakes us out of bed,
Waves trees like banners before us.
Wake. Look. Adore

Glory.

Resurrection Flower

You place a resurrection
Flower on my desk, an explosion
Of yellow blossom from a green
Stem. All winter it was buried
In the dirt, covered with snow,
Soaked by rains, companion to
Earthworms. Easter in a
Daffodil: Christ leaps up
In your green laughter and light embrace.